Teacher's Guide

by Katya Ferguson

for the

Seven Teachings Stories

a series by Katherena Vermette

Portage & Main Press gratefully acknowledges the financial support of the Province of Manitoba through the Department of Sport, Culture and Heritage and the Manitoba Book Publishing Tax Credit, and the Government of Canada through the Canada Book Fund (CBF), for our publishing activities.

Printed in Canada by Rapido Books
Design by Relish New Brand Experience

The series Seven Teachings Stories is published by HighWater Press, an imprint of Portage & Main Press

Teacher's Guide for the Seven Teachings Stories

ISBN 978-1-55379-705-0

www.portageandmainpress.com
Winnipeg, Manitoba
Treaty 1 Territory and homeland of the Métis Nation

Contents

Preface

This guide is designed to help teachers in early years classrooms use the collection of Seven Teachings Stories, developed by Katherena Vermette, with their young learners. The stories illustrate by analogy the teachings and beliefs of the Anishinaabe, who refer to them as the "Seven Sacred Teachings," the "Seven Goodlife Teachings," and the "Seven Grandfather Teachings." Although the concepts are described in this guide as the Seven Teachings, it is important for us as teachers and for our students to recognize the spiritual aspect of the teachings.

In language that is accessible even to very young children, each story follows a child who is exploring the complex nature of how people interact with one another and with the world. The main characters learn that the ethics of a good way of life are revealed as love, wisdom, humility, courage, respect, honesty, and truth.

Within this guide, you will find a framework and key ideas for using the stories with readers. They present an opportunity for educators to become participants in a culturally responsive classroom community and to deepen their understanding of the teachings. The stories open up a space to discuss diverse perspectives, experiences, and traditions with children, and to foster a deeper understanding of ourselves as human beings and of our relationships with others.

Although the Seven Teachings Stories are designed primarily for readers in kindergarten to grade 3, they could be used with readers at other levels. Beginning readers would benefit from teacher support such as in small-group guided reading and through scaffolded conversations that help reveal the deeper meanings in the stories. On the other hand, older students or more proficient readers could benefit from reading these texts on their own or through literacy processes such as a Literature Circle or book club.

You are encouraged to be creative, using this guide in flexible ways that suit not only your own teaching style but also the needs and interests of your learners. It's important to know your own students and, with that knowledge and your creative input, make the teachings come alive in your classroom and your community.

This guide is presented in three sections:

- Part 1: "Seven Teachings for Teachers" offers suggestions and pedagogical approaches to provide a framework for teachers using the stories in an early years classroom.
- Part 2: "Teaching the Stories" presents each story sequentially in a chart format. The Title and The Teaching of each story appear at the top of the chart, with a mini reproduction of the cover. Of the two sections below, the right section provides key information under the headings Topic, Anishinaabe Vocabulary, Story Characters, and Story Summary. The left section, "Guiding Comments and Questions," provides suggestions to guide student learning.
- Part 3: "Strategies and Activities Applicable to All Stories" offers approaches and suggestions that teachers can apply to any of the seven stories — to deepen children's understanding of the abstract concepts addressed in the stories. Relevant classroom materials (CM) mentioned here can be found in the Appendix.

Portage & Main Press 2015. *Teacher's Guide for Seven Teachings Stories*. ISBN: 978-1-55379-705-0

PART 1
Seven Teachings for Teachers

LOVE | ZAAGI'IDIWIN

"Having a love for students means a love for the potential of all students.... It is difficult to hold low expectations for those you love."

(Morrell 2013, p. 155)

- It is important to frame our own teaching within the context of love (Morrell 2013). We can do this by holding high expectations for all learners. We will likely have many emergent and struggling readers in our classrooms in the early years. However, it is important to honour their ability to think deeply about personal and social issues.
- Love is at the heart of all things and a baseline for committing selfless acts to help others (Toulouse 2011, p. 42). This reminds us about the importance of making meaningful connections with our students and of constantly affirming their potential. Humanize the learning environment to help all kids feel good about themselves as learners and as people (Morrell 2013, p. 156).
- Our students need to feel safe and cared for, and they need to form meaningful attachments based on trust in order to learn and develop. As Ernest Morrell reminds us: "This is not an extra, it is actually necessary in many cases for the transaction of learning" (Morrell 2013, p. 156).

Portage & Main Press 2015. *Teacher's Guide for Seven Teachings Stories.* ISBN: 978-1-55379-705-0

WISDOM | NIBWAAKAAWIN

> *"As critical teachers, we must be aware not just of local issues, but also of national and international events and topics shaping the world and our students' lives, either directly or indirectly."*
>
> (Morrell 2013, p. 157)

- Wisdom is about asking questions, observing with the heart, and developing a curiosity about the world in order to develop as conscientious citizens (Toulouse 2011). As teachers, we like to have a clear outline for what we will teach, but this statement reminds us that we need to approach our teaching with an openness to listening and observing our students and honouring their personal inquiries.
- These books connect to social studies and language arts curriculums across Canada. Look at local curriculum documents in your province or territory for additional teaching resources that offer instructional suggestions for linking the story to learning objectives at the appropriate level.
- Make connections to students' real lives, to local issues, topics, or events that are shaping the world in which we live. Use the teachings as lenses for analyzing particular issues that the children care about and to make the teachings relevant and engaging. Such discussions can help students find their voice as advocates of social justice.

HUMILITY | BEKAADIZIWIN

> *"As teachers, we also need to be critically reflective about who we are and our beliefs and ideas about education and young people because they shape what is done in the classroom."*
>
> (Morrell 2013, p. 157)

- Humility, according to Anishinaabe tradition, refers to one's ability to know oneself as a sacred being with both strengths and limitations, and the ability to ask for help when needed in a way that is gentle and insightful (Toulouse p. 46).
- Teaching and learning are very personal acts. We need to acknowledge our strengths and challenges and encourage our students to do the same. Approaching teaching and learning with humility and an inquiry stance can unify the class in common purpose.
- Seek the advice of Elders, Knowledge Keepers, and indigenous consultants in your local province, territory, or nation.
- With interested colleagues at your school, consider discussing the Seven Teachings Stories in a Professional Learning Community, or exploring indigenous perspectives in grade groups or during whole-school professional development days.

COURAGE | ASSKODE'EWIN

"Bravery is the ability to conduct oneself and treat others with integrity — that is, not to be afraid to stand up for what one believes in (that which is equitable and just)."

(Toulouse 2011, p. 48)

- When the seven teachings are not part of teachers' personal tradition, they might hesitate to introduce the stories or to use other indigenous frameworks because their own knowledge is still developing. We do have a responsibility to develop an understanding of indigenous history and beliefs in classrooms of all age levels.
- It's important to recognize the high degree of importance that some indigenous nations accord to the Seven Teachings, and to explore how they correlate to similar beliefs within many creeds.
- Embrace the challenge. Give the children the opportunity to explore the similarities and differences of the world views and perspectives of others as well as their own. With today's technological communications at our fingertips, we also have greater access to indigenous resources, all of which increase our ability to incorporate a wide range of cultural viewpoints.
- We, too, need courage to take the risks that move our own professional learning and teaching forward.

RESPECT | MINAADENDAMOWIN

"Respect is a key determinant in one's commitment to equity and valuing other cultures."

(Toulouse 2011, p. 43)

- Foster a classroom climate that respects and embraces multiple viewpoints and worldviews.
- These books are not just for indigenous learners — they are for all learners to nurture mutual respect and understanding.
- We understand the importance of activating prior knowledge and making connections to previous experiences, content, or ideas. Approach the Seven Teachings within the framework of the stories and consider:
  - How do these connect to other cultural teachings?
  - How are these similar to or different from other sacred teachings or traditions?
  - Do we see evidence of how these teachings are being used — or not — in our daily lives?
- Consider contextualizing the Seven Teachings as a framework for your classroom agreement to foster mutual respect.
- As you work through the stories week by week, continue to use the common language of the teachings in everyday classroom conversations.

Portage & Main Press 2015. *Teacher's Guide for Seven Teachings Stories*. ISBN: 978-1-55379-705-0

HONESTY | GWAYAKWAADIZIWIN

"Honesty refers to a person's ability to be open-minded and candid in a respectful way in daily interactions. Honesty is the internal measure and/or inner voice that lets someone know what is right and what is wrong."

(Toulouse 2011, p. 50)

- Be mindful of the range of texts and learning resources in your school and classroom libraries. Ensure that they provide honest representations of the diversity of cultures and languages among your student population.
- Historically, indigenous peoples' traditions and worldviews have been misrepresented or purposely omitted from the learning materials available to schools. Young readers soon lose interest when they rarely or never see themselves reflected in their school's resources.
- In recent years, the texts representing indigenous groups and written by indigenous writers have increased — an important and positive change in Canadian schools and Canadian publishing. It is past time for their stories to be told.
- The STS series offers a way to begin a new era of critical and culturally responsive literacy practices, even for the youngest readers.
- We must be sensitive to the effect, positive or negative, that a single story can have on a child's self-image and self-confidence (Adichie 2009). By asking questions, drawing out responses, talking about connections, we allow our students opportunities to develop the language for expressing their honest feelings about story, characters, and concept.

Portage & Main Press 2015. *Teacher's Guide for Seven Teachings Stories.* ISBN: 978-1-55379-705-0

TRUTH | DEBWEWIN

> *"Truth is about living all the teachings in a good and balanced way. It is about knowing what one's role is and following one's dreams with integrity and kindness."*
>
> (Toulouse 2011, p. 51)

- Justice Murray Sinclair, Chair of the Canadian Truth and Reconciliation Commission, notes that the truth of the past was that "schools were about changing the identities of indigenous children" (Sinclair, p. 7). Past aims were not to educate but rather to culturally assimilate by any means possible.
- The Truth and Reconciliation Commission of Canada (2014) calls for teachers to take action in order to restore mutual respect between peoples and nations.
- Justice Murray Sinclair also states: "It is precisely because education was the primary tool of oppression of Aboriginal people and mis-education of all Canadians that we have concluded that education holds the key to reconciliation" (p. 7). Katherena Vermette's Seven Teachings Stories can help you and your students initiate a process of reconciliation.
- Explore ways to use the teachings when discussing short-term and long-term goals with each child, to understand how the teachings can help them to achieve their goals. With the story of each teaching, encourage the children to take action toward being a better friend, family member, and citizen of their local community.

Portage & Main Press 2015. *Teacher's Guide for Seven Teachings Stories.* ISBN: 978-1-55379-705-0

PART 2
Teaching the Stories

This section provides an overview chart for each of the seven stories.

- The heading includes the title, with a reproduction of the cover, and the teaching explored in the story.
- Below the heading, the narrow right column provides at-a-glance Topics, Vocabulary, Story Characters, and Story Summary.
- Prior to reading the story to the children, or with them, familiarize yourself with these overviews, including the topics and the language revealed in the story. Introduce the names of the characters and the new vocabulary, and discuss them with the children.
- The bulleted left section of the chart provides Guiding Comments and Questions.

Portage & Main Press 2015. *Teacher's Guide for Seven Teachings Stories*. ISBN: 978-1-55379-705-0

THE TITLE

The Just Right Gift

THE TEACHING

A Story of Love

GUIDING COMMENTS AND QUESTIONS

- Discuss aspects of the story before reading it. Hold up the cover, and ask the children to predict what the story might be about. Name the main character and spell out his name on a chart. Ask them to suggest what word they would use to name the four images above Migizi's head.
- Turn their attention to the picture on page 3, the "photo" of Migizi and his Gookom, and tell them the name for the young boy, Migizi, who loves his Gookom, the Anishinaabe word for grandmother.
- Discuss other names for grandmother: What do the children call their grandmother? Write the different names and add other names for family members on the chart.
- Ask: What do you think Migizi and his Gookom appear to be doing in the photo? After the discussion, ask: What would you write as the caption to the photo?
- Have you ever wanted to find something for someone in order to show them you love them? What was it? Why did you choose it?
- Have you ever given someone a hug to make them feel better? How did you feel? How did they feel?
- Talk, write, or draw about someone you love. How do you show your love for this person?
- After reading the story, discuss what the teaching about love means to the children. Ask them to sketch or write their response in a writer's notebook.

TOPIC

Family illness

How to show love

ANISHINAABE VOCABULARY

gookom grandmother

migizi eagle

STORY CHARACTERS

Migizi, a young boy

His mom

His sister

Gookom, his grandmother

Mr. Bee, his teacher

STORY SUMMARY

Migizi tries to find just the right gift for his Gookom.

THE TITLE

Amik Loves School

THE TEACHING

A Story of Wisdom

GUIDING COMMENTS AND QUESTIONS

- Before reading the story, look at the images of the animals on the cover. To activate their prior knowledge, encourage the children to talk about these four animals. How do they imagine the animals might figure in this story?
- The first few pages introduce Amik's feelings about school and learning. Make connections to your own feelings about school and learning, and ask the children to describe theirs.
- Give prior notice to parents that you will be discussing residential schools with the class when reading this story. It will be helpful for parents to know in advance because their children will likely come home with comments and questions.
- Consider inviting family members to come to school to discuss this topic from their perspective.
- Discuss the pages in the story that deal with the grandfather's experience of residential school. Infer: When Amik's Moshoom describes what residential schools were, ask the students how they might feel attending a school like that. Do they know any family members who went to residential schools? Why do you think Moshoom did not like his teacher?
- Compare and contrast the similarities and differences between the residential schools and your current school.
- Infer: How do you think Moshoom felt going to Amik's school? What part of the story makes you think that? Did your feelings change?
- Amik shows his Moshoom the different ways he learns at school. Does all our learning and wisdom come from teachers and schools? Connect the discussion to the different ways we learn, grow, and develop. Who are other people who help us? How can our friends help?
- Talk about symbols. Do the animals on the bulletin board in the picture serve as symbols? Where else do we see animals used as symbols?
- After reading the whole story, discuss what the teaching of wisdom means to you at school, at home, and in the neighbourhood?

TOPIC

Residential Schools: This important topic will require additional discussion beyond the conversations to introduce the story.

Smudging

ANISHINAABE VOCABULARY

moshoom grandfather

amik beaver

makwa bear

ma'iingan wolf

migizi bald eagle

miskwaadesi turtle

STORY CHARACTERS

Amik, a young boy

Moshoom, his grandfather

Mr. Bee, his teacher

STORY SUMMARY

Amik loves school but realizes that his grandfather, who went to a residential school, did not have a positive school experience.

To help him heal, Amik takes his grandfather to his own school.

Portage & Main Press 2015. Teacher's Guide for Seven Teachings Stories. ISBN: 978-1-55379-705-0

THE TITLE

Singing Sisters

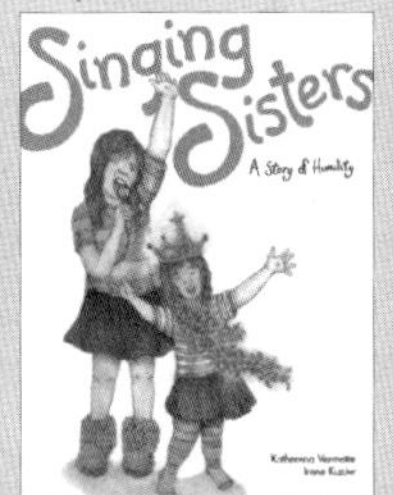

THE TEACHING

A Story of Humility

GUIDING COMMENTS AND QUESTIONS

- Prior to reading the story with the children, discuss the words the children know for a range of family members. Introduce the word "siblings," which covers brothers and sisters.
- Connect: After you have introduced the main character's name and pronunciation, discuss with the children whether they have older or younger siblings, and ask them to describe how they feel about them.
- Once into the story, ask the children: Have you ever felt like Ma'iingan or her little sister? Was there a time when you were upset because a sibling was doing something that you knew you were good at?
- Make an inference about why Ma'iingan might not want her sister to sing. How did this make her sister feel? How do you know?
- When does Ma'iingan demonstrate humility? Find an image or page and describe how this demonstrates the teaching of humility.
- After reading the whole story, discuss with the children what the teaching of humility means to you. Have them offer their own interpretation.
- Draw ways you can show humility in your family or among friends.

TOPIC

Sharing with siblings

Differences between owning one's talents with humility and boasting/bragging

ANISHINAABE VOCABULARY

ma'iingan wolf

STORY CHARACTERS

Ma'iingan, a young girl who loves to sing

Her little sister

Their mama

Their aunties

STORY SUMMARY

Ma'iingan learns to share the singing spotlight with her younger sister.

Portage & Main Press 2015. Teacher's Guide for Seven Teachings Stories. ISBN: 978-1-55379-705-0

THE TITLE

The First Day

THE TEACHING

A Story of Courage

GUIDING COMMENTS AND QUESTIONS

- Once you read the first sentence of the story, ask: How do you think Makwa feels going to a new school? Did you have this experience when you started at a new school?
- Ask the children to share some of their worries and concerns when they started at a new school, or moved to a new home.
- Why doesn't Makwa want to let go of his Mama?
- Makwa's Mama reminds him of all the times he was brave. Make a list, or sketch, or share all the times when you were brave.
- What helped Makwa feel comfortable? How do you think he will feel when he comes back to school tomorrow? What makes you think that?
- If you saw someone come to school feeling like Makwa, what could you do or say to help them feel welcome and included?
- Makwa's Mama says, "Being scared is part of being brave." Ask the children to reflect on this statement and then discuss their feelings. Do they recognize that someone can be scared and act bravely anyway?

TOPICS

Moving to a new school or to a new home

Social inclusion

ANISHINAABE VOCABULARY

amik beaver

makwa bear

misaabe giant

STORY CHARACTERS

Makwa, a very young boy

His mama

His daddy

Mr. Bee, the teacher

Misaabe, a boy at school

Amik, a boy at school

STORY SUMMARY

Makwa is nervous about going to a new school.

When his Mama reminds him of times in his life when he showed bravery, he develops the courage to stay in school.

Portage & Main Press 2015. *Teacher's Guide for Seven Teachings Stories.* ISBN: 978-1-55379-705-0

THE TITLE

Kode's Quest(ion)

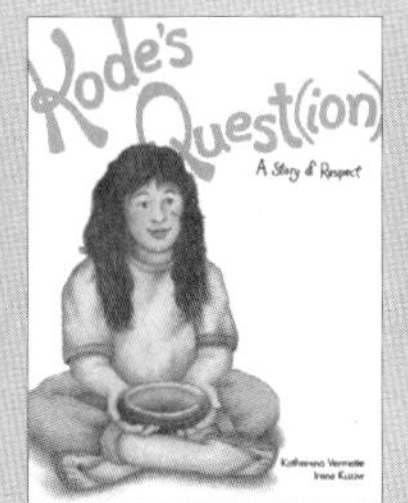

THE TEACHING

A Story of Respect

GUIDING COMMENTS OR QUESTIONS

- Before reading, predict what this book might be about. Analyze the title of this book. Why does this book title, *Kode's Quest(ion)*, include parentheses? Discuss the two words "quest" and "question" and how they relate to one another.
- Ask children to look at the cover of the book. Ask: "What do you think Kode is holding in her hands?"
- As Kode goes on her quest to learn more about respect, she asks different people in her life. Each member of her family shares a different perspective, and Kode has to think about this for a long time. Invite the children to share how they show respect to family and to others. For example: Kode's dad says, "Respect is when we treat Mother Earth well." Discuss the ways in which you treat Mother Earth well and with respect.
- Suggest the children go on their own quest to learn more about this teaching. They might ask family members, friends, or others about what respect means to them. What do the meanings have in common? What are the differences?
- Look at the image (on the pages before the last page) of Kode and Betsy, the cultural teacher. What are they holding? How does this image connect to the teaching of respect?
- Talk, write, or draw about someone you respect. How do you show respect for this person? Have students act out scenes where they show respect in different contexts.
- After reading the story, discuss what the teaching of respect means to you.

TOPICS

Quest, questing, questioning

Smudging

Sage

ANISHINAABE VOCABULARY

mashkode-bizhiki buffalo

nidede dad

nimaamaa mom

nimise sister

gookom grandmother

mishoom grandfather

nisaye brother

nimishoomis my grandfather

nookoomis my grandmother

STORY CHARACTERS

Mashkode-Bizhiki (Kode, for short), a young girl

Nidede, Kode's dad

Nimaamaa, Kode's mom

Nimise, Kode's sister

Nisaye, Kode's brother

Nimishoomis, my grandfather

Nookoomis, my grandmother

Betsy, the cultural teacher

STORY SUMMARY

Kode goes on a quest to figure out what "respect" means.

She asks many people in her life to help solve this mystery.

Portage & Main Press 2015. *Teacher's Guide for Seven Teachings Stories.* ISBN: 978-1-55379-705-0

THE TITLE	THE TEACHING
Misaabe's Stories 	A Story of Honesty

GUIDING COMMENTS AND QUESTIONS

- Discuss Misaabe's feelings about reading. How does he cover up his true feelings?
- Why do you think Misaabe lied to his friends about reading books and about his dad? How do you know?
- Discuss the importance of being creative and using one's imagination. When is this helpful? When might this become a problem?
- Represent a true story about yourself. Then, practise creating and representing an imaginative story in order to develop an understanding about the difference between fact and fiction. It may also help to sort books in your classroom library based on these categories.
- What happens when Misaabe is honest with his friends?
- Why is it important to be honest?

TOPIC

The difference between fact and fiction, truth and lies

ANISHINAABE VOCABULARY

ma'iingan wolf

misaabe giant

migizi bald eagle

amik beaver

STORY CHARACTERS

Misaabe, a young boy

Ma'iingan, his friend

Migizi, another friend

Amik, another friend

Mr. Bee, the teacher

Mom

STORY SUMMARY

Misaabe tells great stories, using his imagination. Soon he begins to recognize that, when he is honest with himself and others, he can still be interesting.

Portage & Main Press 2015. *Teacher's Guide for Seven Teachings Stories*. ISBN: 978-1-55379-705-0

THE TITLE

What Is Truth, Betsy?

THE TEACHING

A Story of Truth

GUIDING COMMENTS AND QUESTIONS

- Before reading the story, ask the children — or remind them — about the role that Betsy has in the school. Discuss the title *What Is Truth, Betsy?* with the children. Continue to the story's first page and note the use of italic font for emphasis on the word *is* in Betsy's statement "Truth just *is* (italic)" and her follow-up question to Miskwaadesi "What *is*?"
- Miskwaadesi answers Betsy's question "What else?" by saying, "We *are*. We're all good people, and we should try to live in a good way. Some people are broken or need help, but we're all good inside. We were all babies once." "*We are*" gives the assurance that people are real, that we exist along with the animals and elements in nature — and that Truth, although not visible, can also be real.
- Ask the children to offer other "truths" as you list them on the chart.
- Discuss with the children the illustrations of the sweat lodge and Thunderbird House on the middle pages. Ask if they have seen these before, and invite them to share their connections.
- Discuss the images of people drumming and singing. Do they have a connection? Do they know how to drum? Can they sing any special songs from their community? Invite the children to share their knowledge with others.
- After reading the whole story, discuss with the children what the teaching of truth means to them and discuss your own meanings and understandings of truth.

TOPIC

The Medicine Wheel:

- the four directions,
- the four colours
- the four sacred medicines

The sweat lodge

Drumming

Ceremonies

ANISHINAABE VOCABULARY

Anishinaabe the people

Anishinaabekwens an anishinaabe girl

miskwaadesi turtle

STORY CHARACTERS

Betsy, the cultural teacher

Miskwaadesi, a young girl

STORY SUMMARY

Miskwaadesi discovers truths all around her.

PART 3:
Strategies and Activities Applicable to All Stories

STRATEGY TITLE/DESCRIPTION	HOW-TO
Shared writing (whole group) Create a "found poem." A found poem is free-form poetry created by using words or phrases found in and selected from another text. (Ray 2006)	• Have the children look through the illustrated pages to choose words and phrases that catch their attention. Write them on sticky notes, and place the sticky notes in a pocket chart or on a whiteboard. • Working together, arrange and re-arrange the words and phrases until the poem sounds the way the students think it should. • Read it together and revise it as needed. Keep it in the classroom as a shared reading activity. • Creating a "found poem" in this way can also serve as part of "word work" or spelling activities. • Encourage students to use other topics or texts and work as partners or in small groups to "find" other poetic phrasings and create found poems.
Make connections Text-to-self, text-to-text, text-to-world. (Keene and Zimmerman 2007)	• Introduce an image, a phrase, or an idea from any of the stories. • Encourage the children to discuss their personal connection, how that connection relates to another image or story, and why it might be important to their world.
Image-to-image connection	• Ask children to choose an illustration from a story that connects to their life. Have them draw their own picture to show the connection. Encourage children to bring in a photo from home or take digital photos of images relevant to the story they have been reading.
Analyze character names	• The names of several characters in the seven stories are the names for the animals that represent the seven teachings. For example, in *Amik Loves School*, Amik seeks to understand the teaching of wisdom. His name in the Anishinaabe language means "beaver" and represents "wisdom."

Portage & Main Press 2015. *Teacher's Guide for Seven Teachings Stories*. ISBN: 978-1-55379-705-0

STRATEGY TITLE/DESCRIPTION	HOW-TO
Tell your name story	• Ask parents to share their name stories with their children and invite them to the classroom to tell these stories. This could become a great literacy activity to connect home and school. • A name story could answer questions like: ▪ Am I named after someone in my family? ▪ Does my name come from the natural world? ▪ Is my name a blend of two family names? ▪ Does my name have a meaning in another language?
Analyze issues related to each of the seven teachings (See CM#1 in Appendix.)	• Consult with the children to choose an issue that matters to them, their school, or the community. Examine that particular issue through the lens of several teachings. • Use the "gradual release of responsibility model" (Pearson and Gallagher 1983) or the "optimal learning model" (Routman 2005) in order to scaffold the process for the children. • First, model this strategy with the children. Use it again as a shared writing activity or within small-group reading circles. Work toward having the children do this activity as independent work. • See the completed example (CM#1B) for reference.
Medicine Wheel (See CM#2 in Appendix.)	• Use the framework of the Medicine Wheel to organize the children's thoughts, ideas, and responses to deepen their understanding. • Use and/or adapt the format (CM#2) to serve your specific learning focus. You might organize it around elements of story — character, setting, problem, solution — and one of the teachings. • You might look at four events or four quotes from different characters and ask: "What do these events or quotes tell you about the character?"
Venn Diagram (See CM#3 in the Appendix.)	• Use or adapt the blank format (CM#3, Venn Diagram) to serve your specific learning focus. • Suggestions: Compare and contrast two characters from different stories. Compare two different stories. Compare two different teachings.

STRATEGY TITLE/DESCRIPTION	HOW-TO
Act out the story	• Select one of the stories you have read and talked about with the class. Ask the children to work with a partner and choose scenes they want to act out. • Create tableaux based upon different images or events in the story.
Create story vines	• This strategy focuses on the development of oral language skills and fluency. Create a story vine (McKay 2008) using objects, pictures, and text that the children can hold or reference to support their sequencing and retelling of the story. • Encourage the children to choose one of the stories for retelling, using a story vine. Support the children who have chosen the same story within a small group. • Invite readers to create their own story based on one of the seven teachings. • Provide multiple opportunities for the children to practise, share, and celebrate their stories with peers, adults, and families.
Questioning for deeper understanding	• Model the process of asking questions about the cover or about images from the story. Then do a "picture walk" and encourage the children to ask questions that prompt reflection and deeper understanding. For example, they should try to ask open-ended questions that do not have a clear yes or no answer. • Provide question frames to help support children's oral language development (i.e., I wonder if…?).
Create "identity texts"	• Create opportunities, such as in Writer's Workshop, for children to write and create their own story for one of the seven teachings, a story that reflects their own identity and experience. • "Identity texts refer to artifacts that students produce. These texts (written, spoken, visual, musical, or combinations in multimodal form) hold a mirror up to the student in which his or her identity is reflected back in a positive light" (Cummins 2006). • Identity texts may include a variety of multi-modal texts – songs, masks, photos, collages, poems, sculpture, and dance.

Thoughts on Anishinaabe Culture and Language

KATHERENA VERMETTE

The Seven Teachings Stories are intended as a small introduction to the ancient teachings of the Anishinaabe people. When introducing the Seven Teachings to students, many teachers are unsure where to begin. I wrote these Stories from my own beginning place, when I too, had to introduce these large, abstract concepts to my very young students and wasn't quite sure how to do it.

I started where I would advise everyone to start: I asked an Elder for help. Over the next few months, we had countless entertaining conversations with our students as we all tried to understand what big concepts like humility or respect could mean. The Stories were born from those conversations and are completely inspired by my wonderful students. Yet they are suitable for all children who are trying to make sense of very big ideas. Often, I have found that non-Indigenous teachers are reluctant to approach Indigenous cultural concepts for fear of offending or making a mistake. My advice, first and foremost, is to seek out an Elder or Knowledge Keeper in the community and ask for guidance. The dialect may be different than the one used in these books, and the teachings may be interpreted differently in other territories, but it's the Elders who are the authority in every community. Go forward with humility. Do not be afraid to admit what you don't know, learn alongside your students, and ask questions together.

Language

The vocabulary in the stories comes from the Anishinaabemowin in this part of the world – Winnipeg and southeastern Manitoba. Anishinaabe, also sometimes called Ojibwe, is grouped by linguists in the Algonquian language family.

Patricia Ningewance, the language expert who guided the language process in my stories, is from Lac Seul First Nation in Ontario. As one of the world's foremost authorities on the Anishinaabe language, Patricia uses the double vowel system with the most updated spellings. This is considered to be the authoritative version, but differing dialects, historical spellings, and many individual words do vary across the Anishinaabe territories. I cannot thank Patricia enough for her guidance when we used this system in the Seven Teachings Stories, and for her dedication to the Anishinaabe language.

Language loss is a reality in many indigenous communities, and my own

Portage & Main Press 2015. *Teacher's Guide for Seven Teachings Stories.* ISBN: 978-1-55379-705-0

history is no exception. I am only a student of this very old and very complex language, and I approach it with great love and respect. My pronunciation, however, is only adequate because, somehow, I always have a French accent. My language teacher was generous enough to never laugh at me; instead she smiled and encouraged me to keep going… and practice.

My advice to non-Anishinaabemowin speakers is to do the same. Own up to your lack of expertise, and find resources in your community or online, and practice. Ask your students how their loved ones pronounce these words, and learn the different dialects. I was a novice in my own classroom and taught only simple words under the guidance of a Traditional Teacher – we called this "language exposure." We took small steps, and planted seeds that would, we hoped, foster future language development.

The language used in the Seven Teachings Stories contains the names of the animals representing the Teachings, and are also the names of the children. We also used some family names to provide another group of words to learn. Together, they provide beginner's steps in becoming familiar with this beautiful language – like the Stories that offer only a beginner's insight into vast, ancient cultural concepts.

Anishinaabe Words in the Seven Teachings Series

FAMILY RELATIONSHIPS	ANIMAL AND PERSONAL NAMES	WORDS WITH SPECIAL MEANING
gookom grandma **moshoom, mishoom** grandfather **nidede** my dad **nimaamaa** my mom **nimise** my older sister **nisaye** my older brother **nimishoomis** my grandfather **nookoomis** my grandmother	**amik** beaver **migizi** bald eagle **makwa** bear **ma'iingan** wolf **kode** (short for Mashkode – Bizhiki) buffalo **misaabe** Big Foot, or sasquatch **miskwaadesi** turtle **anishinaabe** the people **anishinaabemowin** the Anishinaabe language	• smudge, smudging, smudge pot • sweat lodge • healing • ceremonies • the drum • the four directions: North, South, East, West • the four basic colours: white, black, yellow, red • the four medicines: sage, sweetgrass, tobacco, cedar

References: Patricia Ningewance, *Talking Gookom's Language,* <www.patningewance.ca>; *The Ojibwe People's Dictionary*, < http://ojibwe.lib.umn.edu/>

Portage & Main Press 2015. *Teacher's Guide for Seven Teachings Stories*. ISBN: 978-1-55379-705-0

References

Adichie, C. N. 2009, October 7. Chimamanda Adichie: The danger of a single story [Video file]. Retrieved July 10, 2015, from <https://www.youtube.com/watch?v=D9Ihs241zeg>.

Cummins, J. 2006. "Multiliteracies pedagogy and the role of identity texts." In *Teaching for deep understanding: What every educator should know*, pp. 85–93, edited by K. Leithwood, P. McAdie, N. Bascia, and A. Rodrigue). Thousand Oaks, CA: Corwin Press.

Keene, E., and S. Zimmerman. 2007. *Mosaic of Thought: The Power of Comprehension Strategy Instruction*, 2nd ed. Portsmouth, NH: Heinemann.

McKay, M. 2008. *Story Vines and Readers Theatre: Getting Started*. Winnipeg, MB: Portage & Main Press.

Morrell, Ernest., R. Dueñas, V. Garcia, and J. Lopez. 2013. *Critical Media Pedagogy: Teaching for Achievement in City Schools*. New York, NY: Teachers College Press.

Pearson, P. D., and M. C. Gallagher. 1983. "The instruction of reading comprehension." *Contemporary Educational Psychology* 8: 317–344.

Ray, W. K. 2006. "Exploring inquiry as a teaching stance in the writing workshop." *Language Arts*, 83(3): 238–247.

Routman, R. 2005. *Writing Essentials: Raising expectations and results while simplifying teaching*. Portsmouth, NH: Heinemann.

Sinclair, Murray. 2014. "Education: Cause and Solution." *The Manitoba Teacher*, 93(1): 6–10.

Toulouse, P. 2011. *Achieving Aboriginal Student Success: A Guide for K to 8 Classrooms*. Winnipeg, MB: Portage & Main Press.

Truth and Reconciliation Commission of Canada. 2014. *Honouring the Truth, Reconciling for the Future: Summary of the Final Report of the Truth and Reconciliation Commission of Canada*. Retrieved from <http://www.trc.ca>.

Appendix

Instructions for Classroom Materials

CM#1: Analyzing Issues Using the Seven Teachings

- The Medicine Wheel has an internal circle in the centre with the heading "Issue" and the word "Teaching" at the topmost of each quadrant.
- Ask your class to describe a problem or issue that matters to them, and write it in short form in the central circle. Discuss which of the teachings could help them resolve that issue.
- Write one of four relevant teachings in each quadrant. Work with your class to analyze their particular issue through the lens of each teaching they choose.

CM#1B: Example: Analyzing the Issue of Bullying

- This Medicine Wheel provides an example, using the issue "Bullying at recess" chosen by one class.
- The text shows the summary points and questions raised and discussed by the class.

CM#2: Medicine Wheel

Teachers find they can use this format of the Medicine Wheel in many ways:

- to focus discussions of story elements such as character, setting, problem, and solution
- to focus discussions of how the teachings can overlap and show different viewpoints on an issue
- to look at four different events from each story
- to choose meaningful quotes from different characters in each story

CM#3: Compare and Contrast: Venn Diagram

- Provide a copy of CM#3 for use by small groups or a pair of children to use.
- Have the children talk about and describe two different characters, or different stories, or different ideas or topics that they would like to compare. Have them write the two elements for comparison on the lines above the left and right circles.
- Model how to compare and contrast: Write the similarities (shared elements or characteristics) in the overlapping middle sector of the two circles.
- In the larger part of each circle, write the important differences.

Portage & Main Press 2015. *Teacher's Guide for Seven Teachings Stories*. ISBN: 978-1-55379-705-0

Name:______________________________ Date: ____________________

Analyzing Issues Using the Seven Teachings

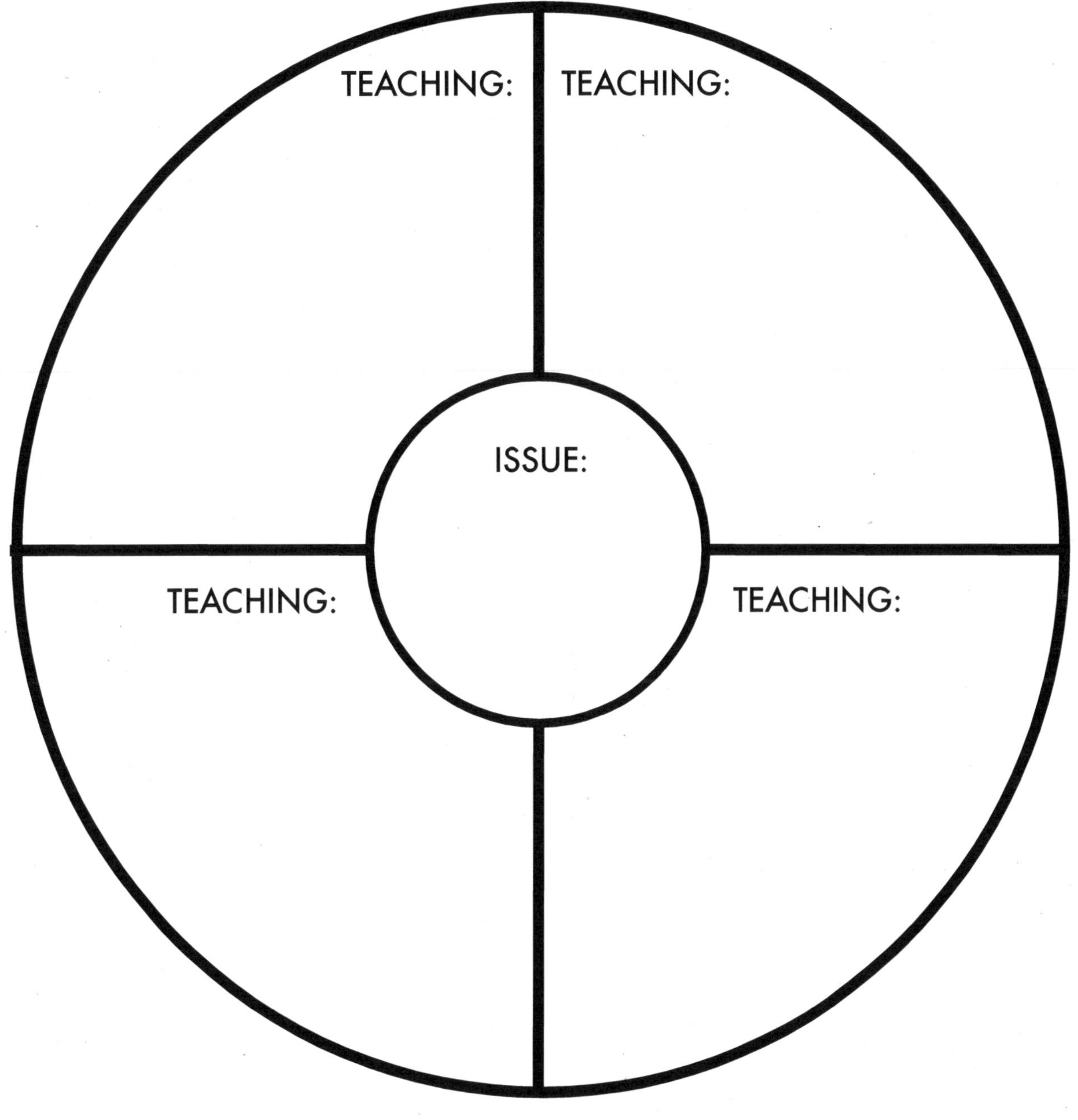

Example: Analyzing the Issue of Bullying

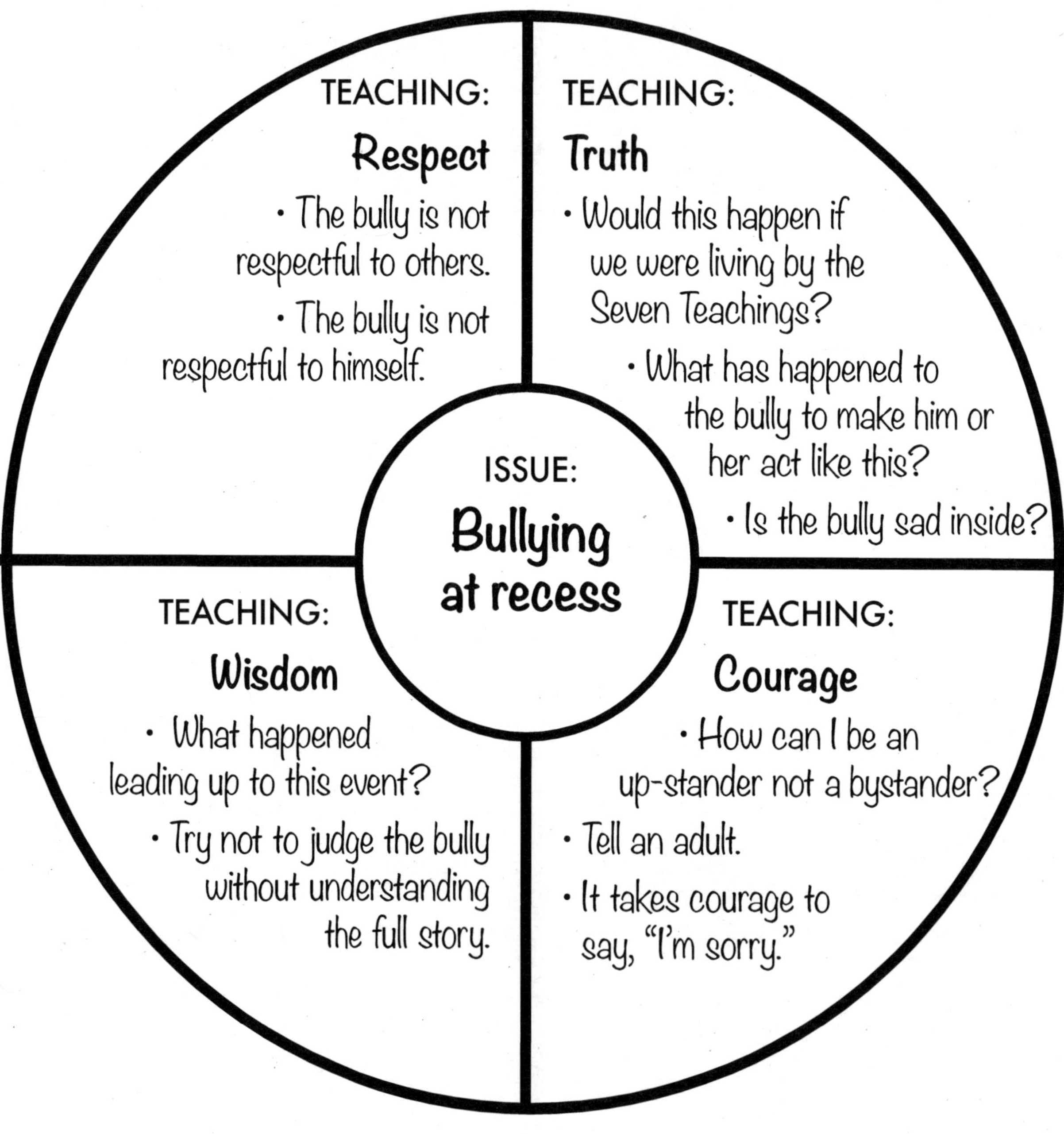

TEACHING:
Respect
• The bully is not respectful to others.
• The bully is not respectful to himself.
TEACHING:
Truth
• Would this happen if we were living by the Seven Teachings?
• What has happened to the bully to make him or her act like this?
• Is the bully sad inside?
ISSUE:
Bullying at recess
TEACHING:
Wisdom
• What happened leading up to this event?
• Try not to judge the bully without understanding the full story.
TEACHING:
Courage
• How can I be an up-stander not a bystander?
• Tell an adult.
• It takes courage to say, "I'm sorry."

Name:____________________ Date:____________________

Medicine Wheel

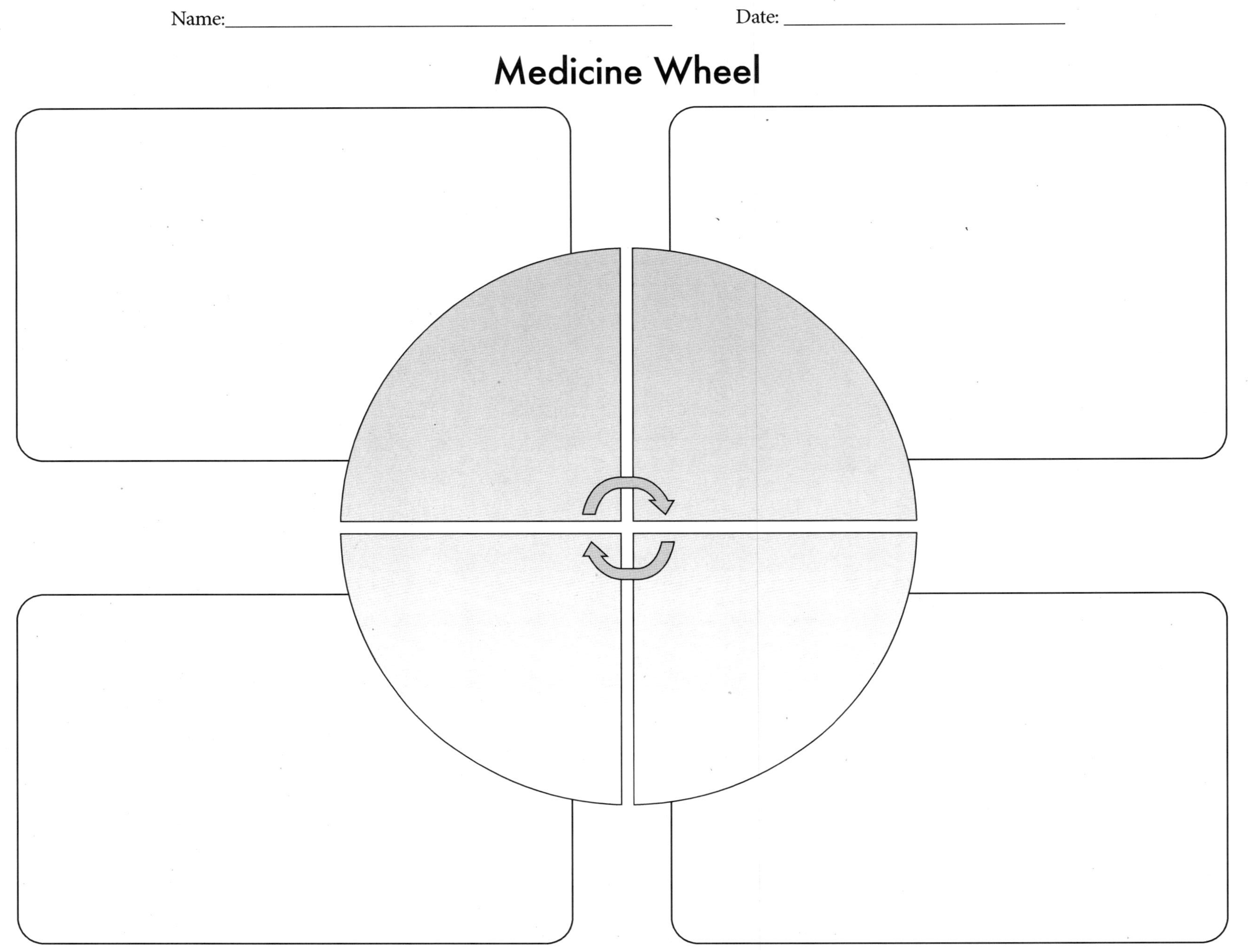

Portage & Main Press 2015. *Teacher's Guide for Seven Teachings Stories*. ISBN: 978-1-55379-705-0

Name:______________________ Date: ____________________

Compare and Contrast : Venn Diagram

______________ Both ______________

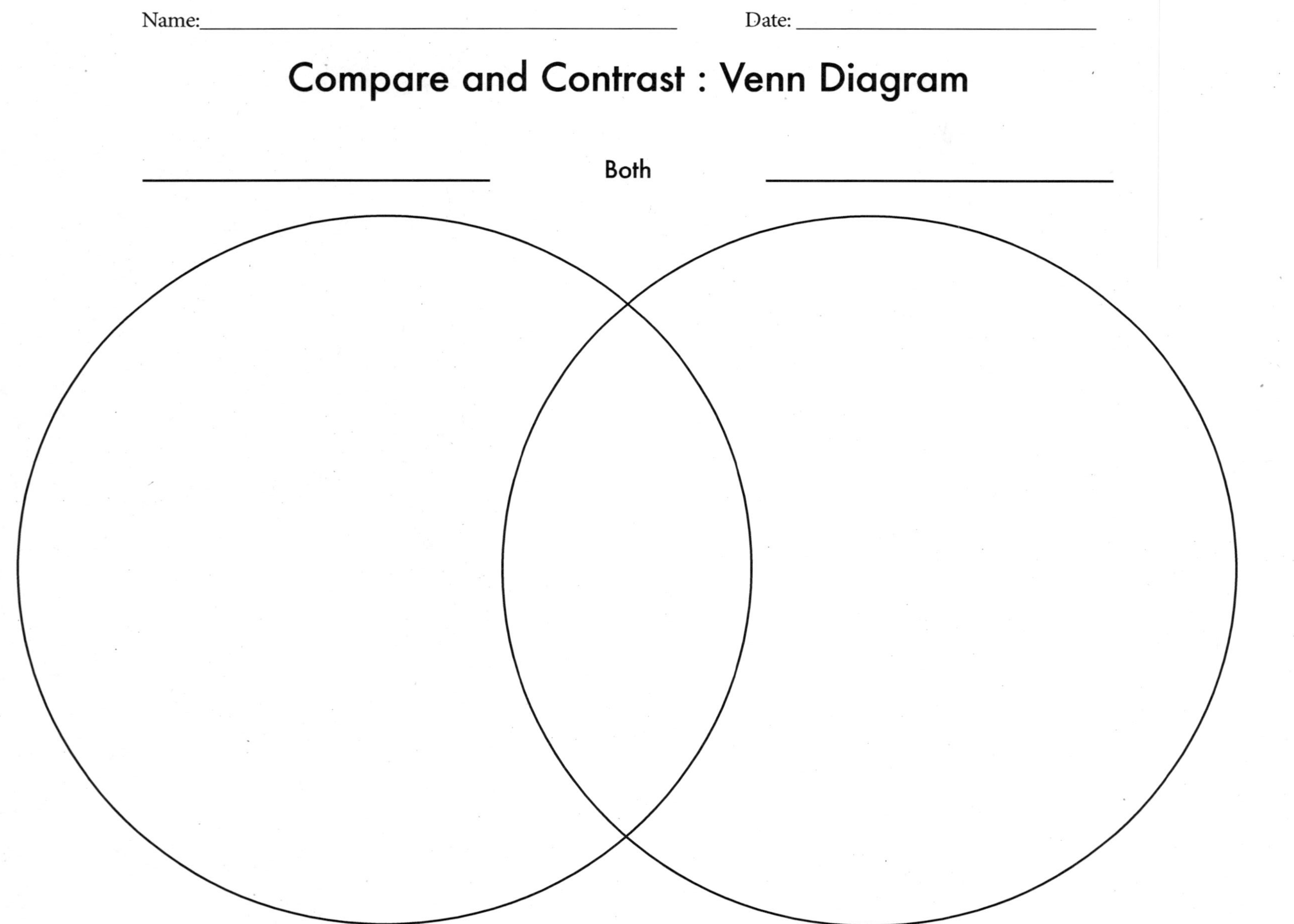

Credit: CM#3 is reprinted from page 63 in Appendix A of the *Teacher's Guide for the Series Tales from Big Spirit* (2014) by David Alexander Robertson, published by Portage & Main Press.